HOW TO SURVIVE A GATOR ATTACK:

THE SUBTLE ART OF NOT GET-TING CHEWED ALIVE

Bill Kilpatrick

Manufactured in the United States of America
Copyright 2018 by Bill Kilpatrick

Library of Congress Cataloguing-in-Publication Data

Kilpatrick, Bill, 1965 -
how to survive a gator attack: the subtle art of not getting chewed alive/
Kilpatrick.
 pages cm
ISBN: B07DNVDZYB
1. Comedy.

For Sherri, who knows more than anyone,
that there's probably something wrong with me.

PREFACE

Typical scenario. You just got to Florida. You're so excited. You've been planning this trip since before they found that lump.

You can't wait to hit the beaches. You're psyched about the theme parks. But before you do anything, a friend wants you to come hang out in swamp country.

That's what we call the rest of the state.

This is when smart people hear the cellos. They've seen this movie before. They've learned not to trust anybody who's missing too many teeth.

So you go.

You're out in the country. You're taking walks through the woods. You're trying to forget what you've seen in Silence of the Lambs. You see a beautiful, freshwater lake and you suddenly feel the urge to rip off your clothes and dive in.

And that's when it happens. You get eaten by a gator.

This is so embarassing. You told yourself you weren't going to let this happen. No, not you. You'd heard of the idiots who came down here, looking for trouble – and found it.

You remember people telling you this vacation would cost you an arm and a leg. but you didn't think they were being literal.

How could you let this happen?

Wake up and smell the mildew. This is the real world, pal. Shit like this happens all the time.

One minute you're getting Mickey's autograph. Next thing you know, you're missing your pen and the hand it was in.

They're in the belly of the beast, who doesn't care who you are. You were dumb enough to wander into his backyard.

Now, not all of you is going back. You came for Spring Break and you got it with a vengeance.

That's why I'm here. I'm not from Florida. I moved here in high school. I'm from Arizona. Arizona doesn't have alligators, except at the zoo.

I'm here to help you leave the state with the same number of fingers and toes you came here with.

Say what you will about the human hand. It was never meant to be used as a chew toy.

I've been down here for 24 years, looking out for people like you. Every time you hear a story about a tourist who gave this state the finger - the hard way - you can bet he didn't buy my book.

Serves him right.

In the meantime, none of my readers has been eaten by a single gator. Not one.

So, if you're not going to take this advice seriously, stop reading. I don't want you messing up my numbers.

Think of this book as that sign at work, the one that ticks off how many days you and the rest of the team managed to stay out of the hospital while hot-gluing eyeballs onto painted rocks.

Don't make us restart the sign. Nothing is more depressing than

DAYS WITHOUT INJURY: O.

This book is written for people who want more out of life than to end up as gator crap.

RULE #1-THIS IS GATOR COUNTRY

Florida is home to the gators. I know you're thinking, "Isn't it also home to the Seminoles?" Yes, and to the Hurricanes and the Bulls and all that other bull.

Do you want to be funny or keep all your fingers?

Alligators have been around for millions of years, unless you think the Earth is only 6,000 years old, in which case, they've been around for 6,000 years - plus or minus 200 million.

Their group, Crocodylia, has been around for about 84 million years, which is insane if you compute it in dog time.

The gators you see haven't changed much in 8 million years. (Insert Boomer joke here.)

What I'm trying to say is they're really old-fashioned and a tad territorial. They're Florida's oldest seniors.

Like all seniors, they know all the words to, "Get Off My Lawn."

The rest of us are just visitors. In gator time, we just got here. We're party crashers thinking we invented the phrase, "Now, it's a party," but this party was going long before we got here and it will keep going long after we've boarded the rockets or somebody put hantavirus in the chili.

In other words, we're in their home.

And when you're in somebody else's home, it's a good idea to re-member you're a guest and behave like it.

Because at this house, the owner will grab you, drown you, leave you at the bottom and then slowly eat you like a hot pocket.

RULE #2 – LOOK TWICE; SAVE A LIFE:

ALLIGATORS ARE EVERYWHER

There are more than a million gators in Florida. A million. Let those words seep in. *Mill-ion.* That's 17 gators per square mile.

That's a lot of big, toothy lizards, an average of 30,000 per county. This place is crawling with them.

They lay 50 to 90 eggs at a time, so, they're out there.

They're in the lakes and the rivers. They're sleeping in sewer pipes, sunning themselves on the road. They're crawling through drive-thrus and doggy doors, and showing up in swimming pools.

You might want to watch where you step.

But there are also 21 million Floridians. That's 362 per square mile.

Human beings - and I'm using that term loosely - are everywhere. They breed like flies, chop down the woods, drain the swamps and drive over everything.

They replace gator habitats with shopping malls and gated communities and trailer parks.

If I were a gator, I'd be watching my step.

Human beings are a dangerous breed. They outnumber gators 20 to 1 and they've been known to stab them and shoot them and run them down.

Gators make great wallets and shoes. Their heads make terrific paperweights. And if you cook 'em right, they taste like chicken.

Don't ask me how I know this but I do.

A group of gators is called a congregation, something I keep in mind every time I get roped into going to church.

They're social creatures, often sunning together and swimming together. If they did have a church, I imagine the sermon would be about us.

To gators, we're the devil and the end of the world. Actually, that's probably how we look to anything we haven't killed and eaten yet.

For millions of years - or 6,000 if you're reading this in Kentucky - this was their home. Then one day, we showed up, and there went the neighborhood.

In the 50s and 60s, gators were driven nearly to extinction. They were put on the Endangered Species list. It became a federal crime to kill them. Rednecks were furious. Talk about buzz-killing a Saturday night.

But it worked. All that protection gave gators a chance to come back as a species. And baby, they're back, a million strong.

They're no longer Endangered. They've been reclassified as Protected. You can kill a gator but you have to have a thousand-dollar permit.

So gators are everywhere - in all 67 Florida counties.

Whether you're down here to get drunk and tattoed, or you're blowing up a national election, or you've started your own neighborhood watch or you just put your daughter in a garbage bag - there's a gator nearby.

There's a gator for every 10-15 people. Florida gators outnumber lawyers twenty to one.

We're in their house. They live here. We're just tourists.

Fortunately, gators are not like that ex who left you with nothing more than a Post-It note or a text. They know what they want.

Gators like to hang out near the water. They like freshwater. They like marshy areas. They like to make splashy-splashy.

They can't regulate their body temperature, so they're a lot like a five-year-old at night. "Can I get a drink of water?" "I need to go to the bathroom."

You'll find them coming out of the water to sun themselves, then go back into cool off.

When people hear this, they freak out. "Oh my God, am I going to be assaulted by a gator?" That just depends. Do you like to hang out in a marsh? When you see a retention pond, is your first instinct to rip off your clothes and skinny dip? Do drainage pipes look enticing?

When I say alligators are "everywhere," I don't mean they're on your roof. They're not in the parking lot taking up the handicapped spot. They're not at Dollar Tree. They don't surf. They're not big fans of NASCAR.

Part of being a Florida survivor is learning to think like a gator. You can still play *What Would Jesus Do?* Just add an extra dimension to it.

What Would Jesus Do if He Were an Alligator?

Put down your alligator briefcase. Take off your alligator loafers. Put on your alligator thinking cap.

Take a good look at where you are, where you're going and think: *If I were a lizard the size of a Harley, would this interest me?*

RULE #3 – IF YOU SEE SOMETHING; RUN SOMETHING

Alligators are a lot like women (and Confederates). They're territorial. They want their space. If you come too close, they're going to leave a mark. Just refer back to Rule #1 and you'll be fine and dandy.

The female alligators are protecting their nests. I don't know what the male alligators are doing. Maybe they're just assholes. Whatever the case, the closer you get to their teeth, the greater the likelihood they'll be using your arm as a lozenge.

Alligators run surprisingly fast, maybe because they're wearing alligator boots. For short distances, they can outrun you. There's a bullshit tip that says to run in a zig-zag fashion. Bad idea. Alligators corner like a Porsche 911. That's a good way to end up a snack. If you have an alligator behind you, run in a straight line. The sooner you get out of their territory, the better.

Everything you need to know about getting bitten is out there. Just go to YouTube and search for "alligator attacks." It's an endless sea of dopes getting down in the water with them, sticking their hand near their mouths, doing bullfighting shit with a t-shirt and otherwise bringing themselves within snapping proximity of that mouth.

Of course, a lot of people don't understand the concept of the tail. I've met some guys who liked to chase some tail but it never ceases to amaze me how often people will get close to a gator and not suspect that that tail is coming for them.

Alligators use their tails as whips. They use them to knock animals down, which is pretty clever when you consider they have a brain the size of a quarter. Down on the ground is where their mouth is. As a general strategy, I try to keep my head off the ground.

In the water, alligators can get up to 30 mph, though that's more of a lunge than speed boating. They're not fucking marlin. On land, they can lunge pretty fast as well, anywhere from 11 – 20 mph, but it's not so much a hot trot as a quick *I'mGonnaGetYa*.

So, what's a non-Floridian to do? Here's an idea: Don't swim with them. Don't stand next to one. Don't charge one. Don't just stand there. Run away, dummy. Run away.

RULE #4 – UNFRIEND AND BLOCK

Remember all the hubbub about Terri Schiavo? Her husband just wanted her to die with dignity, after she suffered irreversible brain damage. But other folks - including then-Governor Jeb Bush - held out hope she'd get better.

Like she had the flu.

Some people swore up and down, when they looked at her, they could see a hint of recognition. Like she was Sammy Jankis from *Memento*.

After a lengthy battle in the courts, she was finally allowed to die with dignity. Life support was turned off and that was that.

After she died, they cut her open and wouldn't you know it? Her brain was the size of Sean Hannity's testicles. Whatever people thought they were seeing wasn't there.

Hint of recognition my vestigial tail.

And yet, when people look at a gator, they think, "This could be my friend." They look at the 84 million-year-old design, with a brain the size of a quarter, and they see the reptile equivalent of their dog.

No, it's not.

It's the 84 million-year-old equivalent of a bear trap. Stick your hand in there and we'll see who's going home tonight.

It doesn't help that we coddle kids with images of friendly creatures who aren't. Teddy Bears are cuddly. Grizzly bears are not.

If they ever did find a unicorn in the wild, forget about *My Little Pony*. It would be more like *My Little ER Visit: Something Put a Hole in My Chest*.

Cats don't even like us. They're the strippers of the animal world. It's all rubbing, purring and stretching till they get what they want.

Don't ask me how I know that.

I know, you think you can make this work because you own a pit bull that hasn't eaten a baby yet. But with a brain the size of a quarter, that gator doesn't have the hard drive of an Atari 2600.

You just need to tell yourself no matter what you think you see, when you look into its eyes, it's not your friend.

Un-friend and block. This thing only knows how to eat, poop and boink other gators.

It's not that into you. So, wise up, before you find yourself into it.

RULE #5 – THERE'S ONLY ONE WAY TO FEED A GATOR:
JUST ASK ANYTHING SMALL

Listen, Mullet. This isn't 9 ½ Weeks, where you blindfold your girlfriend and dig through the fridge looking for sex toys.

This is a killing/eating/shtooping, pooping machine. That's it.

Fortunately, it's scared of you. You have big legs. You walk upright. You're loud. You listen to Nickelback.

If this thing could dream, you'd be in its nightmares.

That's good. Let it be afraid. Let it stay afraid. Fear is what keeps it over there - as long as you're not dumb enough to go over there.

But you couldn't let well enough alone. You feed your dog and your dog loves you. Maybe this dinosaur from 84 million years ago is just a pitt bull with more teeth.

The moment you do that you start breaking down the fear that keeps both species safe.

I don't know why but people like to feed animals by handing them food. "Hey, Mr. Ed, come nibble this off my palm."

"Hey, Donald Duck, I hope you don't have a problem with gluten because I'm about to hook you up with chunks of Wonder Bread."

Silly people like to show nature that they are some kind of food tray. And that's how you get bit.

Mr. Ed takes a chunk out of your palm. Donald Duck takes a nibble while he's making that weird quackety-quack grunt. Your neighbor's pit bull takes a finger for good measure.

You're an idiot. You thought you could feed the world. You forgot that, in nature, animals don't feed other animals.

Sure, Momma Bird will have the Grand Slam and then puke it up for the chicks, but that's not how it goes for the rest of the forest.

Watch an episode of National Geographic.

In nature, the slow and the stupid "feed" the fast and the furious. Nobody hands a lion a plate or a menu. He just looks up, sees who's having a Monday, and it's Darwin time.

If a gator thinks you're scary, let him keep thinking that.

It's like when my neighbors ask if my dog bites. Well, of course, he does. He specially likes the taste of neighbors who crawl through my window looking for something to pawn.

He's not *their* dog. He's *my* dog. Let them be very afraid. Fear is a useful thing.

RULE #6 – THE BEST WAY TO CATCH A GATOR IS TO MAKE SURE HE DOESN'T CATCH YOU

This doesn't mean you can't come to Florida and spot a gator. Gators are everywhere. Just remember what Bette Midler said about God. Is he watching us? Sure, from a distance.

There are lots of places where you can see gators and have your fun – and it won't cost you an arm and a leg.

Florida is full of zoos and theme parks that have gators and gator exhibits. A lot of lakes are known for gator-spotting spots.

I dare you to say that fast.

The thing to keep in mind is that gators are a lot like some Floridians: Interesting to look at, interesting to talk about, but dirty, disease-ridden, nasty and vile.

There's nothing like a hand full of salmonella to turn finger food into poison.

Remember what your mother taught you when you were two, then when you were three, and again when you were four, five and six: Look but don't touch.

I have a Nikon with a 300mm zoom lens. It puts me right in the gator's mouth without putting me right in the gator's mouth.

You know what they say: A picture is worth ten fingers and a whole lot of toes.

I've never met a gator who chased me down the paparazzi. If you don't mess with them, they won't make a mess of you.

RULE #7 - WHEN ALL ELSE FAILS, FIGHT FOR YOUR LIFE

E very now and then, despite their best efforts, somebody ends up with a part of their body inside a gator's mouth. How you handle this will affect the rest of your day.

Good luck trying to pull those jaws open.

When you bite into a piece of steak, you do so with a force of about 100 to 150 pounds per square inch. Lions bite with about 1,000 psi. A gator bite is about 3,000 psi.

That's the equivalent of getting bitten by 30 toddlers simultaneously. "Sure," you're thinking, "I've taught preschool before. I can handle this."

No, you can't.

I don't care if you swim with a crow bar, you ain't going nowhere. Not unless the gator wants to open his mouth.

Your job, should you find yourself in this situation, is to get the gator to open his mouth. Y

You got to give him a good enough reason to do so.

Professional gator wranglers - also known as idiots - have a trick they use. If they have any reason to think they're about to get bit, they grab the gator and hold his mouth shut.

Talk about hacking mother nature!

You see, gators are way better at shutting their mouths than opening them. The whole jacked-up, spring-loaded muscle-popping design is geared toward snapping shut, like a trap, with bone-crunching force.

Mother Nature never thought about what to do if some Crocodile Dundee jumped a gator and held his mouth shut. The muscles that open his trap are surprisingly weak - or at least nothing like the walnut cracker he uses to bite with.

So, that's one answer, though not a very good one if he's already got you by a body part you know you'd miss.

It's not like you can kick 'em in the balls. That would totally work with me (It has in the past) but I'm not 9 to 15 feet long. Unless you're really leggy, you're talking about the wrong end.

And what do you do if it's a female? It's not like you can give her a titty twister and hope she gets offended.

Experts have basically come up with three options, none of them great but beggars can't be choosers.

First, you can poke them in the eye. Contrary to popular belief, gators have good eyesight. They ought to, with those big eyes strapped to the sides of their heads.

This gives them an advantage as they hunt for their prey.

But it's not such an advantage when you go hunting for an eye. Gators have really big eyes, which make them easy targets if you're in the eye-poking business.

But there's a catch, no pun intended.

Gators also have a certain mobility when it comes to the eye. They can actually "suck" them back into their skulls when they feel threatened.

Remember that time your kid brother scarfed the Jell-O into his face like it was chasing something down his throat? Gators do that with both eyes.

That could make for quite an experience as you try to go all Uma Thurman on that eye.

And while eye gouging sounds like a great idea on paper, keep in mind that your hand or arm is in the gator's mouth, so you're going to have to come at it with your free arm.

But that's likely to be the one further away.

If this is a big gator - and you're in a world of pain with your heart about to explode - getting to that eye may be easier said than done.

So, we go to option number two: Punch 'em in the face.

Believe it or not, this is an awesome option. Like sharks - and your brother - the nose is a tender spot to clobber. Gators may be covered in body armor, but that nose is their glass jaw.

People have actually broken free from gators by smashing them in the nose.

Walloping that shnozz not only lets you play Pop Goes the Weasal but it freaks out the gator, just as it does with a shark or your brother.

Many are the time when a gator has gotten somebody in his clenches, got popped on the nose and decided he was getting too old for this crap.

The typical gator reaction is to swim away, muttering profanity and concluding you wern't worth it.

But there's also a third way, one pioneered by a little girl: Stick your fingers up the gator's nose.

I'm not kidding.

I don't know why this works but it does. I don't know if it hurts or if the gator feels violated but four out of five gators surveyed prefer you not do that.

You know what they say. You can pick your friends. You can pick your nose. But you can't pick your friend's nose.

Nobody has ever gotten eaten by a gator after giving one the finger in a place he least expected it.

It's also not a bad idea to lose your cool and swear like a sailor. While you wouldn't want to do that in a situation where you could retreat, if parts of you are stuck in the bear trap, what have you got to lose?

Lots of creatures go all Blow Fish when they need to. It's one of the few reasons animals growl and make noise.

You want to do something before the gator rolls you over, as drowning is his modus operandi. He (or she) means to pull you under, drown you and then store you as a food supply to keep coming back to.

Just knowing that would make me go berserk.

This reminds me of the time my dad took us across the country for work. The company's home office was in Denver so we ended up stopping in a small town, in the foothills of the rockies, looking for breakfast.

Dad was partial to mom-and-pop diners, so we were in this little town, walking around the "downtown" area, on a Sunday morning that was eerily quiet. The streets were silent and vacant.

It was like an episode of the Walking Dead.

And then this killer bloodhound popped out of nowhere, barking and woofing and growling. Everybody was on edge.

That included Dad, who was wired for sound, about as tightly packed as a golf ball - and that was on a good day. Right about now, he came out of his skin.

"YOU BETTER SHUT THE HELL UP YOU MOTHERFUCKING SON OF A BITCH BEFORE I PUT MY HAND DOWN YOUR THROAT, GO THROUGH YOUR ASS, GRAB YOUR TAIL AND PULL YOU INSIDE OUT!!!!"

Now, that was a performance.

The dog shut up and walked away and we didn't have another issue with him. But somewhere, hanging over the rockies to this very day, is a spate of profanity so harsh it makes the angels cry.

So, if you find yourself, with your arm in a gator's mouth, unable to gouge him in the eye and forced to finger his nose or bash it something furious, there's nothing wrong with going berserk while you do it.

Give him the old Mel Gibson.

What have you got to lose? He'll never take your freedom.

THE BIG WRAP-UP

GIVE IT TO ME STRAIGHT

A lot of people say they'll never come to Florida, not if it's crawling with gators. They've seen Jurassic Park. They know how the movie ends.

But gators are a minor issue. We are the real threat. We're chopping down the woods, draining the wetlands, poisoning the air and drinking up the water.

They are the ones more likely to be run over, stabbed, shot, poisoned and driven into extinction. They're scared of us and they stay away from us for a reason.

But they also have a brain the size of a quarter.

Like a lot of humans, courtship is in April while May and June are time to get jiggy. If these wetlands are rocking, don't come a knocking.

But knocking is exactly what we do best. We go tromping into what's left of the Florida woods and stumble into their territory, and then we blame them when it all goes sideways.

Then it's all, "Stand-your-ground, POP, POP, POP. A license? What's a gator license? He started it."

Florida gets about seven alligator attacks a year. Your chances of getting injured are about 2.7 million to one.

In my case, the odds are even more astronomical, as I sit here writing this, sipping away at my Coke and soaking up the AC. I don't live on a lake or a river. I take hikes in the woods but I don't wade into the tall grass hoping to find a friend.

I respect gators. I don't mess with them and they don't mess with me.

But if you're a snow-shoveling American, thinking of taking a trip to Florida, and keen on not getting mauled, drowned and turned into gator chow, here is a quick run-down of the tips we talked about:

1. Alligators live here. This is their home. The rest of us are just visiting.

2. Alligators live on or near freshwater. They're in the lakes. They're in the rivers. They're in the grassy wetlands near the lakes and the rivers.

3. Alligators hunt and live in the waters but come out to sun themselves. They don't like to wander too far from the water but they do go back and forth to regulate their temperature and build their nests.

4. Gators court in April and mate in May and June. That's their vacation season. It's a great time to spot them. It's not a great time to tromp around their nests.

5. Female gators are particularly protective of their nests.

6. Gators are not blind. They can see quite well with those great big eyes. But when conditions are dark or murky, they can mistake you for dinner.

7. Gators are scared of people so they generally stay away but not if you feed them and not if you corner them or threaten their nests.

8. As gators are territorial, stay out of their territory.

9. Gators can swim faster than you. They can also run you down, at short distances, so if you see one, back off.

10. If a gator is chasing you, forget about the zig-zag crap. Just run. The quicker you get out of their territory, the better.

11. If a gator bites you, forget about prying open those jaws. You're in there till he lets go.

12. Getting grabbed by a gator is a serious deal, not just because of the jaws and the teeth but because gators will roll you over and drown you, so you want to act fast.

13. You can't kick them in the balls, but you can poke them in the eyes, punch them in the nose or stick your fingers up their nose.

14. Nothing says you can't go berserk and do your best Mel Gibson impression. This is your party, baby. Put up a fight.

15. After the attack, seek immediate medical attention. Make sure you clean that wound and wash thoroughly because you've just been to the Salmonella store. (Did I mention that Florida is also home to flesh-eating bacteria?)

16. If you do get bit by a gator - and I mean this from the bottom of my heart - get back on the plane. You're might be too dumb for Florida, which is a life-changing revelation.

17. There are exceptions to every rule. I know nothing. I just thought this would be a fun book to write. If you did get bitten, it was probably the gator's fault. You probably locked horns with the one gator who just doesn't read books like this.

18. In Florida, your chances of being a victim of a violent (human crime) are 1 in 232. In 2016, Florida had about a thousand murders, seven thousand rapes, twenty thousand robberies and sixty thousand assaults.

19. Florida is also a great place to get jacked, with about 100,000 burglaries, about 400,000 thefts and more than 40,000 car thefts. Almost none of these involve gators.

20. No humans were harmed in the making of this book, although my heart rate did go up when I thought about what I would do if a gator had my arm.

ABOUT THE AUTHOR

Bill Kilpatrick is a stand-up comic and a writer, though you wouldn't know that from reading this book. He currently lives in Florida where he stays away from gators.

Made in United States
Orlando, FL
13 December 2022

26473531R00019